# RICOCHET

Two women war reporters and a friendship under fire

**MARY JO MCCONAHAY**

Copyright © 2014 by Mary Jo McConahay

All rights reserved. No part of this book may be reproduced, scanned, or distributed in any printed or electronic form without permission.

First published by Shebooks
Paperback edition through waynegoodmanbooks


ISBN: 978-0-9888143-9-4
Library of Congress Control Number: 2016946384
20160719

# RICOCHET

# RICOCHET

## March, 1989

The plane banked over the surf, came in low over khaki sand, and hit the runway with a single bump, rolling to a stop under the familiar welcome sign:

THE ARMED FORCES ARE PROTECTING YOU

Outside, the heat hit like a sucker punch. It never felt cool in El Salvador, but March broiled, when cicadas cried out by day and nights simmered. Elections were scheduled anyway, and the war didn't stop for sun or flood. At least, I thought, I would be working with my best friend, Nancy McGirr, Reuters photographer, who was unflappable. I liked thinking of us as a team.

I grabbed a cab and rolled down the back windows so the breeze blew from both sides. The driver stepped hard on the gas. The airport road was the best in El Salvador, paved and straight, but lonely. I knew the spots—everyone did—where abductions and certain murders had occurred. I never wanted to look out the window on this stretch, but inevitably, I did.

It was a relief to come into sight of San Salvador, sprawling before its mountains like a threadbare version of Los Angeles. There was always something to report on immediately in this city—a strike, a skirmish, an unfortunate but high-profile assassination. Anticipation rose in my throat, honey and bile.

The cabbie turned a corner and hit the brakes. We were trapped in a maze of streets crawling with government soldiers holding M16s across their chests. They looked jittery, in the typically jerked lines of men on urban patrol. Faces painted black, even though it was daytime, they moved like giant roaches, armored in dark, puffed vests, stepping into alleys then back out again, stepping in, backing out. The cabbie twisted the radio dial and whining *ranchero* music stopped. We needed all our senses.

"Just a sweep, I think, *un rastreo*," he said.
"Just let's get out of here."
"*Correcto.*"

He dropped me at the Hotel El Camino Real. The entire second floor of guest rooms had been turned into news offices; even reporters based elsewhere sooner or later came to the Camino as they covered the wars in Central America. In the lobby the air was cool and the crowd of hacks in a party mood: Mexicans, Brits, Frenchmen, Germans, the Belgian video teams, other Americans. I knew them all by this time. *Where is Nancy?*

I worked my way toward the reception desk through encounters of hugging and faux surprise, "Hey, you're here!" As if any reporter would be anywhere else. If we didn't stop the Communists in Central America, President Reagan had told Congress, they would spread north until they rolled over the U.S. border, just a few hours' drive away. Never mind that the Salvadoran war was not a Communist insurrection but a rebellion against tyrants who liquidated anyone—even an archbishop—who spoke for reform. Washington supported the elites. El Salvador was a front line of the Cold War, the biggest news story of the day.

Across the lobby, elevator doors opened and a blonde woman in snug orange jeans stepped out, a worn, green canvas camera bag slung over her shoulder. Long hair, eyes bluer than mine. She strode my way, calling out.

"Hey slut!"

Here she was. Nancy and I had been roommates for years in San Salvador and stayed tight after we moved to places of our own in Guatemala, an hour's flight away.
"There are no rooms left," she said.
"But I have a reservation," I said.
She laughed at the idea, tossing her hair.
"So," I asked tentatively. "Did you get one?"
"One what?"
She pulled a face that said, "You are so tiresome." With Nance there were few encounters not worth drama. "Yeah, yeah," she said. "It's a double." Roommates again.
Nancy's boss passed without a hello, a young American whose shirttails stuck out of his pants. He walked quickly through the revolving doors out to the parking lot.
"What's up?" I asked Nancy.
She launched into a stage whisper for eavesdroppers. "If I tell you, I have to kill you." But her Irish eyes signaled "*boring*," to indicate the assignment was routine.
We hugged. This unnerved me. She would be coming back soon. Nancy was not a hugger. It was not our habit.
"Hey, OK," I said, breaking away.
"Hey," she said, and followed her boss. Through the glass I watched as the two of them drove out of the parking lot and onto the Boulevard of the Heroes.
From the lobby you could hear popping sounds outside. You listened a moment, then decided. It was only simple rifle bang-bang, no return fire, not worth pursuing. Lobby conversations resumed. Over in the bar I saw the Mexican reporters signal for another round.

Upstairs in the freezing guest room I fiddled with the knob of a huge air conditioner mounted under a picture window. In the distance rose a plume of dark smoke. Fighting. Or garbage day. The window glass was hot to the touch. How much money is spent in this tropical land trying to make it feel like Alaska?

I had already written most of the Sunday background story for the elections, so I called the desk in San Francisco and dictated it to an editor who typed as fast as I could read—a prized talent in those days before regular dispatch by computer. There should be no need to write again before election returns came in next day, unless something like a political killing occurred or an armed attack on the ballot boxes. Hanging up, I considered the perennial tripartite question: Eat, hit the bar, or sleep? I dialed room service and said, "Raise the Dead." The hotel chef had invented a special version of *levanta muertos* soup to cure hangovers, but it cleared your head any time of the day, hot broth with leafy greens and red chili peppers.

As I waited I read stories in the local papers, which gave an impression that the tension long ubiquitous in the countryside had come to the city. The election would be a turning point in the war. Right wing parties clamored for military presence at voting stations. If the party aligned with rebels won, the five countries of Central America could count two in-your-face leftist governments—the other was in Nicaragua, where the revolution was ten years old. If the Salvadoran far right won, the party of the death squads would become the government. If the center won—well, there was no center.

I must have dozed off in the armchair after the soup. Knocking at the door woke me. "Nance! Use your key!" I said, but rose to answer anyway.

The evening maid entered to close the drapes against the city at war. Thick window glass covered with a layer of fireproof drapes would mute the sound of any explosion more than a few blocks away. The maid turned down the beds, set the chocolate good-night mints atop our pillows, collected the tray with the remnants of the soup. "*Buenas noches,*" she said, and closed the door without a sound.

She left a clear glass pitcher filled with ice water next to the television set. I watched it perspire into a puddle on the table, each drop announcing how the routine of an international luxury hotel might be maintained religiously while the population lived in fear, even died violently a few feet from its doors. In all the years I had covered El Salvador until then, over a thousand days of generalized blackouts and sabotage, the hotel's swimming pool always gleamed miraculously full of sparkling blue water.

Nancy should just walk in the door. Wearing that exaggerated look of fatigue she liked to summon for effect. Put down the camera bag, flop onto the bed, and kick off the white tennis shoes, squeeze her toes, and say it: "Ooh, my dogs are barkin'." We had known each other for five years, knew each other's routines.

I made a couple of calls down to the second floor. At Reuters they said neither writer nor shooter—an unfortunate sobriquet for photographer—had returned. I called the office that Americas Watch shared with the Dallas Morning News, but Nancy wasn't there either, or at CNN. "No, I'm not worried," I lied. At AP, the radio correspondent said the hall was quiet. It was convenient to have everyone's offices on a single floor when looking for news, a mere sprint up back stairs when the electricity was out. Like a bunker for journalists, the second floor also fed an illusion of safety in numbers.

Just before 7:00 p.m., I took my Sony pocket shortwave from the duffel, looped a wire around the antenna, and fixed the other end to a curtain pull, moving the tiny cable around until it drew in the nightly clandestine rebel broadcast, *Radio Venceremos.* There was news of victorious skirmishes against *el enemigo.* A revolutionary poem. I made myself comfortable in the green leatherette armchair with the radio close to my ear—you didn't want the volume loud—and painted on another coat of nail gloss against a biting habit. From the speaker came an interview with a medic, then advice to voters: *Abstain*. Elections had been rigged, said the announcer, in favor of the right. There was no information about a team of gringo reporters. Nance would come back fine, I told myself, delayed by her boss who fell into a long interview. Or they had stopped for a drink.

Photographers have a tougher time than writers. They run the same risks as we who simply carry notebook and pen, end the same day in the mountains with the same mud on their boots and line of flea bites where their socks stop. But return to the office without a striking picture, and they might as well have stayed home. Worse, they have to expose themselves, get to their feet for the shot, and make their bodies open targets. More than once, Nancy and I had ducked behind a parked car when firing erupted, but it was she who had to raise her head. I curl myself down to the size of the back left tire and don't get up until the birds sing.

She came in at midnight.

"How was it?" I asked.

"Hard to find. Got lost. Went late."

I rolled over and slept again until the telephone rang like a fire alarm, piercing, urgent. Two a.m. I could see the glow-in-the-dark dial of the travel clock on my side of the table between our beds, but nothing else.

I found the lamp switch and got us some light, but Nancy had already answered and was nodding at the phone, saying nothing, which drove me crazy. She should have been making eye contact, covering the receiver with her hand, and mouthing the name of the caller, but didn't.

"Yeah. OK," she said. "*Gracias*."

She looked so unlike herself, pallid, staring at the phone,

that when she hung up I kept my mouth shut. It seemed a long time passed before she said, "Roberto."

The young photographer she had been coaching. I knew the person she meant, by something in the way she said it. Dark floppy hair, sweet-faced. She had been showing him the ropes at Reuters and had told me he had a good eye, would go far.

"That was him?" She shook her head no.

"He's dead."

She walked to the window as if she could see through the drapes. Pivoted and paced to the desk. Returned to sit on the edge of the bed, shaking her head like a swimmer with water in her ears. Silence. You have to wait, let it come.

Roberto had been driving home on a motorbike with another Reuters photographer. Soldiers at the first stop in a double checkpoint looked at their IDs and waved them through; when no one signaled them to stop at the second point, they drove on. Soldiers opened fire. Roberto took two bullets in the back and died on the spot. Somebody found the other photographer tossed behind a dumpster. He had taken a round that came out his chest and shattered his photo-shooting arm, but they thought he would live.

There was nothing to say. "I'm sorry" came up short. You didn't throw your arms around each other and cry, either. You just didn't. Nancy sat for a while with her face in her hands. She slipped back into bed. I turned off the light.

At dawn, reporters flowed out of the elevators, across the lobby, and out the glass doors. Grim-looking. Carrying Roberto's death in their heads. "I'll be working out of the second floor," Nancy had said to me before I left the room.

In the lobby a woman's voice stopped me. "Call me when you get back?" She was a magazine writer from New York, new. No bag, no notebook. Sleek hair, perfectly turned under at the chin line.

"You're not going out?" I said.

She shook her head no, didn't say it was because of Roberto, but for sure it was. She would watch TV reports, use the phone, suck brains when we came back.

"Fine," I said. I thought of Nancy, doing the work of three people all day, in and out of an office on the second floor that felt like a funeral parlor.

Downtown near the university, I interviewed voters in long lines at tables in a park, holding a cassette tape recorder in the same hand as my reporter's notebook, recording in case I needed to check quotes later. I talked to students, professors, market women. Everyone used virtually the same words.

"This voting won't make any difference as long as the war is on," said a father of three who said he went to night school.

"Let's go to Escalon," I told the cabbie. Usually I drove around El Salvador in my 1966 Volkswagen Beetle, but I had left it at home in Guatemala this time. A local cab driver would know the shortcuts on a day when we must move faster than most, keep the engine running should we need to leave a place quickly. We drove north past a statue of the Savior of the World, *El Salvador*, standing on a silver orb in the middle of a traffic island.

In a country with a greater population density than India, the streets of the neighborhood called Escalon, named for a military president, felt spacious, quiet. Gardens bloomed with yellow roses, and window boxes displayed the plant called *Corona del Cristo*, Crown of Christ, thorny stems bearing delicate flowers as red as blood. Tents in telltale United Nations blue stood in several driveways. Friendly governments had rushed them in after the 1986 earthquake to house the indigent homeless, but the flow of Salvadoran corruption had channeled them here, where wealthy residents used the shelters as carports.

A silver-haired man in a crisp white shirt told me he had voted for the right wing party. "The country needs a strong hand against the terrorists," he said. "Terrorists" was code for the leftist opposition, armed or not, or sometimes for anyone who belonged to no camp at all. The year before, trying to reach civilians in a guerrilla-held zone, Nancy and I had been attacked by army mortars as we crossed a shallow stretch of the Torola River in a bright orange rental car; a subsequent investigation showed officers referred to us as *cheles terroristas*, blonde terrorists.

I wanted to survey one more precinct, across town. The driver ignored stop signs. "Makes it harder for the snipers," he said. He pretended he was joking.

You knew you were coming into neighborhoods that favored the rebels when the streets began to crumble. Potholes. No sidewalks. Residents were street vendors, sweatshop workers, low-paid teachers, or unemployed people. As with the earthquake aid, government attention respected only party allegiance, so not much help rained down here. I told the cabbie to wait. I walked unpaved paths among unpainted houses, where gardens were geraniums in coffee cans and an occasional mango tree.

Voters stood quietly, avoiding my eyes and, it seemed, each other's. One young man talked only after I turned off the tape recorder and promised not to use a name. He looked worried afterward anyway, as if his words might come back to haunt him. The pattern repeated. This collective demeanor, fearful and suspicious, was information, too.

"Votes here will not count," said a weary-looking woman wearing an apron.

"Then why stand in these lines?"

"It's against the law not to vote," she said.

All of a sudden, everyone around us looked up. A heavy-set Mexican newsman I knew was chugging by. He saw me.

"*Bomba*," he said, tossing the word like an informational flyer, without breaking pace.

I fell in. Jumped over broken paving stones. Past dogs so thin their ribs showed through like marimba keys. It wasn't clear to me whether we were loping away from a bomb, or toward one. The Mexican reporter stopped midblock, before an open doorway.

The house looked like its neighbors but smelled like a barbeque. We stood on the stoop and peered inside. It was a small room, and from the doorway we could see everything. A young male body sprawled on its back, forearms gone, face and torso blackened. No furniture. Only a table in splinters.

The Mexican reporter, I'm sure, was asking himself the same questions. Was this a bomb lab? Was the dead man making it? Or did he come upon the rig and try to defuse it? The Mexican looked at me and shook his head, "No." He meant don't even think about stepping inside. As if I would.

In the yard, in the street, neighbors knew "nothing." The Mexican reporter took off. If the dead man had looked American or European it might have been a story. But he looked like a local. So the scene became just one among thousands in a war, a death unnoted.

My editors expected me to cover the elections, considered hard news. I promised mentally to return another day and write a feature story about how the violence tore at ordinary Salvadorans like the family of the young man blasted apart, whoever he was. But the vow to come back was really a way to give myself permission to leave the scene. I had made the vow before, and sometimes I did return, believing deaths of locals should matter as much as those of a combatant or U.S. adviser. Mostly, I did not return. Journalists are blown off track in the smoke and rush of wartime just as others are. The shame of it eats into the bone. I have never been able to shake the guilt of what I did not do.

It was time to check election returns at the hotel and find out what was happening elsewhere. Telephone booths and telegraph offices were targets of destruction; obtaining information meant driving to a place and observing with one's own eyes and ears, or on a day like this one, touching base at the Camino. As I neared the cab, however, I saw young people walking out the door of a small house, some in tears. I approached the threshold by instinct, intending to remain unobtrusive. But mourners who were crowded just inside noticed and made way, raising high their white candles, easing me forward.

In the center of the room, a woman rested her head on a long, open wooden box, one arm thrust across it in embrace. She lifted dark eyes as if unseeing, her skin so drained of blood it seemed she herself was no longer among the living. She turned again to the coffin, like a body sinking under water.

Someone took my elbow and guided me to view the deceased. There lay Nancy's colleague, Roberto. I had had no idea where he had lived.

I started to gasp but smothered it. This created a strangling sensation. I realized that those gathered were thinking that I was a colleague of Roberto's purposefully come to pay respects, not some reporter who had wandered in out of curiosity. I shared laments as long as I could, shook hands with each person on the path back to the door. In the open air I walked until I figured no one from the house could see me, bent over between bushes, and retched.

Back at the hotel, there was news. Two more journalists had been killed. The army believed that the press supported the enemy. Not every day in El Salvador was like this one. But yes, some days were so terrible you felt you must concentrate to breathe.

"Can I debrief you now?"

It was the new reporter from New York, her pageboy still perfectly styled. She acted as if we actually knew each other instead of merely having shared a table at breakfast one morning when the café had been crowded. I kept my face blank so I wouldn't sneer.

"I guess you're not going back out," she said. Her expression said she had been right not to leave the hotel, hadn't she?

A German freelancer approached. "Numbers are in," he said.

The candidate of the right-wing party whose founder had established the death squads was the new president of El Salvador. Reports said during polling 46 people died, 63 were injured. The U.S. ambassador called the elections "a civic fiesta." I dictated the story to San Francisco. We did not know it then, but the death squads' party would govern the country without a break for the next 20 years.

When Nancy came into the room a few hours later, she slipped the camera bag from her shoulder to the bed. She looked ragged. "I'm in for the night," she said. She sank into the green leatherette chair, kicked off her shoes, raised her feet to rest on the air conditioner.

I took out my stash of miniature airline whiskies, perhaps a dozen that I had collected on trips, and set them in a line along the diameter of the table. I settled into the other chair and split one bottle between two glasses.

"Your eyes are red," she said.

"Yours are, too."

We toasted without words, drank, and I poured the next small bottle. Eventually we talked, desultorily. I would leave in the morning. She would fly out in a few days when a replacement came in from Mexico City. We lived only 40 miles apart in Guatemala, she in the capital, Guatemala City, I in the colonial town of Antigua, but some months we saw each other most often on the job in Nicaragua or El Salvador. It didn't matter. Whenever we met we picked up wherever we had left off.

After an hour with the ridiculous bottles, abiding the infernal dull whir of the air conditioner, conversation became a disjointed string of single sentences. Separated by long silences.

Then Nancy blurted it out. "I just can't take another picture of a dead body."

Outside, the city was quiet, as if soldiers, rebels, candidates, troublemakers—all were exhausted, too. I had never heard Nancy say something like that.

"Yeah, I know what you mean," I said.

"No, I mean it," she said. Stared right at me. Jaw set.

*I just can't take another picture of a dead body.*

"There is a war going on," I said.

Actually, there were three wars going on—in El Salvador, Nicaragua, and Guatemala. That wasn't counting Honduras, occupied by U.S. airmen and CIA-trained paramilitary troops, a kind of terrestrial battleship from which the U.S. Embassy ran the *contra* war against the leftist Sandinista government in Nicaragua. We were on the job in Central America, I said.

"Dead bodies are central to the theme."

If a photographer doesn't take their pictures, she might as well be somewhere else. I said all this not unkindly, just talking, a dam against her words.

After each shot we put the empty back in place. The line of tiny bottles shone warmly, a file of amber shards.

I told myself not to worry about Nancy. She might take a break but would never quit. Journalism is not a job but a blood type, fate and identification, and we had the same stuff in our veins. Besides, the longer you reported this particular story, it seemed, the closer you came to it. Detaching would be like turning your back on voices you would still hear, on people who figured you were speaking for them. Or in Nancy's case, it would be like turning your back on people who figured you were showing what their lives had become, putting a human face on the headlines.

In that frigid room, a memory returned to me, of a sunny morning at our shared house in San Salvador, when I had opened the door to an old Indian. "They killed one of the *jovenes*, one of our young men," he had said. "The photographer, where is she?" He had traveled by bus to the capital, dressed in the clothes some men still wore in the countryside, a loose, white cotton shirt and white pants that hung short of the ankle, leather sandals.

"The grave is open," he said. "We are waiting for her, *la fotografa*."

We jumped in my Volkswagen. He remembered us, said the old man, because we had done a story some months before on an indigenous religious ceremony that he attended. Soldiers stationed near the village occasionally took potshots at their youngsters, he said. "They suspect we sympathize with the rebels. Or maybe they think it is correct to shoot at us because we are Indians."

The bullet that killed the youth might have been a ricochet or deliberately aimed, but in any event, everyone knew no soldier would pay. In the graveyard, Nancy took pictures of the corpse wrapped in a sheet, the handsome face open to a cooling breeze. Elders standing around,

Pipiles, descendants of Indians who had migrated from ancient Mexico before Columbus, seemed to want that some record of their young man in death might exist in the wider world. As we drove away, they were lowering him into the grave.

In the hotel room at the El Camino Real, I looked across the bottles at Nancy. I shouldn't have to remind her of that day. It was in our collective memory bank.

"You're sad," I said. "I am, too."

She nodded her head yes, then shook it side to side. She was pale. Maybe she was thinking of Roberto Navas, because they had worked together. Or the other two journalists, Cornel Lagrouw, a Belgian, and Mauricio Pineda, another Salvadoran, shot while following the rules on roads we took regularly but happened not to take this day.

"You're tired," I said.

"No."

She let her head fall forward, long hair swinging. The empty bottles scattered and lay like so many fallen toy soldiers. Let them be, I thought. *Just let everything be for now.* When she lifted her head again, she changed the subject.

Under our chairs, however, under the several lower stories of the hotel and out back under the waters of its crystalline swimming pool, I felt something moving. The tectonic plate under our friendship had shifted. Together we had locked eyes under fire, almost drowned as mortars sounded overhead, smuggled medicine for a good cause, been captured by soldiers in a guerrilla zone. I could not imagine reporting the war in a virtual sea of men without her.

"Gotta get to bed," I said. "Up early."

"Yeah," said Nancy. "Wake me up. I'll have some coffee with you." Both of us laughed. "Or not."

# RICOCHET

Nancy and I always disagreed over when and where we met. She said it was in early 1984 after I spoke on a San Francisco panel of journalists, titled by the sponsoring professional organization, "A Year of Living Dangerously." I remember the event for the mendacious romanticism of its name and for a verbal spat with the only other woman on the panel, who insisted a man might have a family and report war but a woman could not. But not for meeting Nancy. Instead, I think we met a month later at the El Camino Real in San Salvador, over breakfast, when we hatched a plan to cover something together that day—a prisoner exchange, if I recall. I liked her right away.

Besides our shared Irish background and Catholic upbringing, which meant we might leave reams unsaid, we talked easily about the fluff of life, jewelry—Nancy once designed necklaces, but we rarely wore them now, and only earrings that didn't dangle—and about clothes, even though our daily dress had become jeans and multipocket vests from Aca Joe's or the original Banana Republic on Polk Street in San Francisco, where stock was global military surplus. And we talked about men, although our tastes were different, which meant we could offer unbiased opinions and were never, that I know of, attracted powerfully to the same man. Both of us were taken by the story we covered, but also by the beauty of the place where we lived. By scenes glimpsed driving from one town to another, between firefights and press conferences, on patrol with troops or guerrillas in the mountains, scenes you longed to immerse yourself in it but couldn't, not yet. Moments like coming over a hill to see a vast valley filled with a million yellow daffodils, the very place where God created daffodils, a beckoning yellow sea you wanted to dive into but must not, keeping instead to the edge where low trees provided camouflage. And soon, the ocean of flowers was behind you. In a place where indulging in beauty seemed always just out of reach, and you wanted a friend to watch your back, Nancy was there.

    After the El Salvadoran elections, after returning to my Guatemala house, I spent weeks refusing to believe she was going to quit, to turn her back on the story, on the sacrifices our colleagues had made. That she was going to leave me.
    "I'm taking evening classes in Thai cooking," she said to me one day by phone. I could hardly believe what I was hearing. What did such frivolity have to do with the life of a war reporter? She spoke of lemongrass and varieties of rice, and I listened as I might to an unfamiliar language. "The chef is quite well known—we make the meal, then eat it together," she said. Over the weeks, she spoke of new friends I had never met, embassy staff and operatives of aid organizations, members of that softer circle of foreigners, as I considered them, mostly Americans, who lived more safely, outside our ring of reporters, different from those of us who were constantly rubbing our noses in the grim pot of the place. When I met Nancy's new friends I felt uncomfortable with them, as if I had to watch my language. I listened to discussions of topics that interested me not at all, like food or where to find the most unusual furniture.
    It was during that time between the El Salvadoran elections of March 1989 and the military crisis point of November, when the guerrillas would launch the final offensive of the war and set its endgame into motion, that nightmares returned. I considered the timing rotten luck: dark spells had come over me before, but why now? Just when I had to worry about the possibility of carrying on alone. When you least expected it, events caught up with you, memory too long tamped down spilled over, of close

calls, of huddling in caves while 500-pound bombs fell outside, of taking cover from helicopter fire by jumping over barbed wire, lightly shredding upper arms, cowering face down, eating dirt. No serious injuries, certainly no worse or even as bad as what others went through, just one's own accumulation of moments of being scared, moments festering below the level of consciousness until they caused a kind of fever in the mind.

Curiously, I thought often of a particular day when nothing had occurred in the nature of news and we heard not a single shot fired. It was a Sunday in 1984, when we had headed out of the capital west on the Pan American highway in the old Volkswagen, whose plates still read, "I'd Rather Be Sailing." The West was silent in a way the rest of the country was not—no firefights, village takeovers, no grand army operations. A friend who was not a journalist, however, a scholar of the region, had told us, "This war you're covering began in the west of the country, trust me." A terrible massacre had taken place in 1932, and I wanted to know more.

Outside the capital, traffic thinned and the highway narrowed. In the distance, volcanoes rose. Occasionally an ox-drawn cart appeared on the side of the road, trundling along no faster than it might have done a century before.

"Do you think anyone will remember what happened 50 years back?" Nancy asked.

"Of course," I said.

"Do you think they will talk about it?"

"Of course."

I thought of the time the Indian elder had come to our door to bring us out to his village, so she might photograph their young man in his burial shroud. So they could tell us how the soldiers had shot him down.

"People want their suffering recognized," I said. Nancy

rolled her eyes as she did sometimes when I made statements that sounded to her *ex cathedra*.

"So you are going to ask them what they saw," she said. "Ask whether they saw anyone killed in 1932. And you expect they will tell you."

"Of course," I said.

Two hours later we drove into the town called Izalco, its sharp edges clear enough to the eye: pastel houses, a central *parque* reliably green, streets running straight to blindingly white churches, Asunción on the south end of town and Dolores on the north. Whenever I have thought of Izalco since then, however, I have thought of a town that lived shrouded, its voice muffled. A place where silence had become so long a habit that you had to strain beyond normal limits to hear the truth of things. The layers of whitewash that covered some walls seemed intended to hide scenes underneath imprinted upon them like images on photographic paper.

We knew Izalco's history from reading the only English-language book on the 1932 uprising of starving Indians, a 1971 classic titled simply *Matanza*, the massacre, written by a historian from Eastern Connecticut State University, Thomas P. Anderson. Inhabitants of the West, mostly Indians, the professor wrote, rebelled against debt peonage and forced migration that split families and ensured plantation labor for landlords and the rich. The insurrection lasted only a few days and failed. Nearly 100 people died at rebel hands; in response, when it was all over, authorities killed more than 20,000 unarmed people, not necessarily because they had participated in the insurrection but because they looked Indian.

We parked under a jacaranda tree blooming with purple flowers near the Dolores church, on high ground, and looked over the town. So steeply did the plain beyond drop to the sea, some 15 miles away, that we could see the line of the blue Pacific. We descended and walked hot streets. From anywhere in town, the view to the north was filled with the indigo mass of a volcano, called Izalco like the pueblo, its sloping walls rising to a peak blown jagged. The mountain loomed like a shadow, inseparable from the town. Remarkably, during the rebellion the volcano had erupted, hot ash falling to mix with the blood on the streets.

We surmised some of the houses we were passing possessed floors once hurriedly dug out to bury Indian-looking clothes or beaded Indian necklaces, as Professor Anderson described. We saw fields whose depths probably hid ordinary tools buried in 1932, lest a man be marked as an Indian peasant by the machete he carried, for example. Residents greeted us with *"Buenos días,"* as you might expect, but seemed to hold eye contact less, to look down to the ground again more quickly than people did elsewhere in the country. I could not shake the impression that the air was denser in Izalco, that the human body moved a nanosecond more slowly than it did in other places. We talked to merchants, a schoolteacher, a tailor. No one, however, even the very elderly, would talk about what happened in 1932. Nancy carried her green canvas camera bag yet took not a single picture, as far as I remember, which was unusual. People in a country at war generally do not enjoy an assumption of privacy, by accident of the place and historical moment in which they live. Izalco, Nancy seemed to think, was different.

In the *parque* across from the Asunción church, a woman who looked about 70 stood with a basket of *guïsquiles* at her feet. I introduced myself, and she did not appear hesitant when I began to talk about the town, asking questions. Hope rose. Nancy listened, but her face did not show the same anticipation I knew mine did.

The woman said she had been born in Izalco, and that, "naturally," she would never forget the month of January 1932.

"The great eruption," she said.

I thought she spoke in metaphor. She did not mention the insurrection, fighting in the streets, or how houses of rich folk were invaded, telegraph offices torched. She looked down at the basket of green *güisquiles*, oblong and spiky, a poor people's food that I quite liked boiled up but that Nancy could not bear, she always said, because it tasted insipid, and she had read it had "no nutritional value."

The woman we spoke with said, "I saw it all, the flames, the ash."

She had never left the town, never in her life, although she vowed to herself, she said, that before she died she would make the pilgrimage to see the Black Christ of Esquipulas, just three hours away by bus across the border in Guatemala. She must remember the days after the rebellion was crushed, I thought, when the army called in residents on the pretense of issuing safe conduct passes. Anyone with "Indian" features, or who had registered as a member of the legal Communist party to cast a ballot in municipal elections (police had the voters' lists), was detained. The thumb of each captive was tied to the thumb of another, and they were marched in groups of 50 to the wall across the street from the spot where we stood now, to face eight soldiers with M3 rifles or old Mausers who fired until all had fallen. Nancy and I had inspected the area around the church but saw no sign or memorial, only the whitewashed wall. I named the dates of the executions and asked the woman with the vegetable basket if she had been in town.

"Yes."

And what had she seen?

"It was difficult to walk," she said. She spread her arms and stepped forward slowly, as if in a trance or sleepwalking.

"Why?"

"The ash," she said. She had no memory of violence, she said.

Town fathers had grabbed two of the insurrection's leaders, a chief of the indigenous religious brotherhood and a member of a respected *evangelico* family, dragged them from jail while the army looked the other way, and lynched them in the park where we stood. Their bodies hung from olive trees for days. So many were slain in Izalco, out of vengeance, their remains could not be buried fast enough or deeply enough, and a putrid odor permeated the air, it was said, well into the month of March.

"For weeks I smelled the air, biting," said the woman with the *güisquiles*. "It was the volcano. Sometimes I think I can still smell it."

Nancy and I returned to San Salvador with me at the wheel, as always, because Nancy doesn't drive. Sometimes the fact that she must always be a passenger bothered me, especially when I was very tired, as if she were not pulling her weight. Besides, as someone who grew up in Southern California and practically slept on the steps of the Department of Motor Vehicles the night before I turned 15 to get my learner's permit, so I could take to the freeways, I could not truly understand the notion of an American woman who did not drive. We were different in many ways, Nancy and I, she from divorced parents and unsentimental about the idea of family, I the oldest of six with parents who still acted like sweethearts; she glamorous-looking with thick blonde hair while I was overly thin, my light brown hair too fine so it never looked neat; but it was the driving I saw—until then—as the real difference between us, something that in the end made little difference at all. That afternoon, however, I was glad to be at the wheel, eyes fixed on the road, returning to earth, because Izalco had seemed to belong in another world, did not fit with what I expected of other people's memories, an experience befuddling.

"Do you think someday we will forget what we have seen?" I said.

"You will when you get Alzheimer's," she said. I must have appeared stricken. Compared with Nancy, I have little sense of irony. "Kidding," she said.

"Bad taste," I said.

"Maybe we won't remember what we don't want to remember," she said.

"If you forget anything, I'll remind you," I said. The sun's last orange rays shone in the rearview mirror as we headed east, into the dark. "And you must do the same for me."

"I told you nobody would talk," she said.

"You didn't tell me, you asked whether I thought they would, and I said yes."

"Yeah. Right," she said.

"And I was wrong."

As I drove, the outlines of an understanding came, much like a photograph emerges in a darkroom, ghostly at first, then clear: memory is fungible. Not only had Nancy warned me of this, implicitly, with her doubt about what we would hear in Izalco. She was a woman inclined to be skeptical, someone who saw with different eyes than I, a check to my mind. She also carried the past I knew, alongside me. *I just can't take another picture of a dead body.* If she quit, there would be no more shared memory.

I was thinking of Izalco late one afternoon as I sat in my Antigua garden, waiting for Nancy to arrive from the capital. Above me hovered the volcano called Agua, a wispy cloud crossing its slopes like a floating communion veil. She had notified Reuters of her resignation, she had told me, effective soon, and she was thinking of teaching photography to kids who lived in the Guatemala City garbage dump. I looked around at yellow gladioli and red anthuriums. Before me vines of orange-pink *camarones*, named for their shrimp-like shape, climbed pale walls to the roof of curved red tiles. Was I missing something in the big picture of our lives, to continue riding a train from which she was jumping? Not only would there be no more shared memory of war. She must no longer value the work we have been doing together, the work I must continue to do, if she is leaving it behind.

Our colleagues, mostly men, seemed to be less interested in what happened to women and children caught in the landscape we covered. I remember exceptions, but that was the rule. I had experienced ordinary mayhem with others, but the stories Nancy and I did together, the ones we felt got behind the war, I didn't do often with other reporters. I thought of her pictures. In a mountain town occupied by child soldiers, a girl of 14 wearing oversized fatigues held an AK-47 semiautomatic rifle, looking scared and defiant at once. Nancy's angle caught the fragile white flower the girl wore in long, dark hair. Another picture, another day, in the capital, a death squad victim slumped over a steering wheel, splintered windshield splattered with blood. Nancy had focused her camera on the face of a young boy looking at the dead man, with an expression that told you all you needed to know about war.

When the doorbell rang I grabbed my bag and met her at the door, because we were late for a cocktail party. On the way, we kept our eyes on the uneven sidewalk to avoid a fall. The air was balmy, but I did not feel relaxed. I did not know why I had agreed to go with her, I said. "You know I hate these things."

"You always say that," she said.

"I mean it."

"Then you always have a good time."

"I won't," I said.

"I told you, you need to relax," she said.

"Hah!"

"We don't have to go, we can just walk around if you want," she said. "I told you, I think you need to talk. How are you feeling? What we see—it's hard, you know?"

"It's *what*?"

"You know."

"We're going," I said.

In the courtyard of our hostess's house, late sun was sapping the bright purple from bougainvillea vines, draining the roses' ardent reds. A dozen of us women, foreigners all, drank sweet red wine and grazed on smoky paté.

"I can't tell y'all how much I love it here already," said the guest of honor, a petite brunette in white shirt and beige pants with a center crease. "I do so feel welcome." She was buying "a little bitty" property to construct a boutique hotel. South of the *parque*, "toward the volcano," she said in a warm Texas accent, demonstrating she was already one of us by explaining directions the Antiguan way.

Inside the house, in a living room hung with indigenous weavings, we settled onto tooled leather sofas, crossed our ankles, and nodded to the maid, who refilled our glasses. Now that she was widowed, said the guest of honor, and still short of age 50, the hotel project and tennis would occupy her time. That, and adopting a baby.

The other guests *oohed* and *aahed*, and voices tripped over each other with advice. Nancy shot me a warning look. I drew back from the table, imperceptibly I thought, but she would not drop her gaze.

"Get a grip," I could hear her thinking. Did she think I could help it?

When we first came to San Salvador, a slight, dark-eyed woman had surprised me in the carport outside our rented house. She held two infants, one in each arm. A girl of about four clung to her skirts. The woman possessed all her teeth, but her forehead was lined. She wore a full apron, as a market seller might, or a woman from the countryside.

She is begging, I thought. Instead, the woman bent forward slightly, opening her arms, holding out the infants.

"Yes, they're beautiful," I said.

They looked alarmingly tiny, however, with eyes closed like new kittens, minuscule fists beating the air, dolls' mouths working. The mother—for that is who she had to be, from the way she gazed at the infants—seemed to read my mind.

"*Sí, son pequeñas.* They are small because they were born only eight days ago. But they are healthy."

I looked around to see if neighbors were watching. The woman drew breath. "Will you take them?"

I looked at the four—mother, babies, little girl—and began to go dizzy. "For no money," she said.

Her husband had been killed only the week before near Zacatepeque, she said, a rural area south of the capital where there had been a firefight. She had no milk to nurse the twins, from the *choque,* the shock of events. And she had to care for the other daughter.

"Three will be impossible," she said.

She held the babies close while making the argument to give them up. I grappled for touchstones. *Sophie's Choice*—no. Perhaps the Old Testament story where Solomon orders the baby cut in half if two women persist in claiming it, so the true mother yields that the child might live? Closer, but not right either. I placed a hand on the Volkswagen's hood to brace myself.

Some neighbor must have told this mother that single

women lived in the house, and we were foreigners at that. She had emerged from under a tree. She must have been waiting, stalking. Resentment rose. This stranger, and perhaps some neighbor, had thrust me into an inhuman situation.

"How did you get here?" I asked coldly.

"Bus," she said.

The girl gripped a piece of her mother's skirt. I wondered if she believed this was her fault, as children will do in a crisis. Or felt at risk of being given away, too. One of the babies whimpered inside its white swaddling, and the woman caressed it back into calm with the side of her chin. I could imagine them, four female souls huddling on a single hard bus seat for hours that morning, bumping their way to the capital. And only two on the return.

At that time Nancy and I had not yet seen fallen corpses. But I knew I was seeing war. I failed the desperate mother, sending her off with money and a dazed wish for good fortune.

I looked across the cocktail table in Antigua through candle flames. The Texas businesswoman bore no responsibility for those infant twins in El Salvador. To believe anything else was absurd. Yet I stared at her and saw a thief. She will claim an infant she has no way of confirming is an orphan. Or with good intentions, she will introduce a comparatively huge, life-changing amount of money (although we will consider its quantity small) into a process with a local woman who likely never had money to call her own.

Nancy glared. I wanted to whisper, "*Whaaat?*"

She and I had seen the same violence, I thought, but she has conquered its memory better, looking elegant now in a fine fuchsia jacket, as if she had never worn clothes caked with brown mud, never counted, for the record, the number of human bodies fallen in a clash. *But I know she has!* How can she quit?

The hostess wanted to draw me into the circle. "You are so quiet."

Nancy reached for her empty wineglass. I crossed and recrossed my legs. I took on a face that said, "*Wow, what would I know?*"

The room breathed out. Nancy leaned her head back on the sofa, and looked like she wished she still smoked.

The maid served coffee, which I took as permission to leave. Nancy caught me up.

"I'll walk you home," she said.

Outside, the remains of a ruined convent looked fearsome by night, sacred stones struck down by a tremor, centuries in the past. Angels who once had watched from cornices lay like corpses in a field. We walked arm in arm on the narrow sidewalk, Antigua-style, past tall walls, hidden gardens. The fragrance of night-blooming jasmine was almost overwhelming.

"You did OK," she said.

"What?"

"I said, you seem better."

When a passing car backfired, Nancy tightened her grip on my arm, but the noise did not make me jump. She regarded me with surprise. "Yes, better," she said.

"I don't want to forget," I said.

"You won't," she said.

Those weeks after the Salvadoran elections felt long, especially when the rainy season began, when time seemed stretched, when every day seemed like two, first hours bright then darkness in the afternoon when the daily *tormenta* rolled in, bringing a deluge that could last all night. The worst thing about these dark spells was that they

# RICOCHET

fogged the eye to beauty, although even at the lowest times I knew it was out there, just waiting to be seen again. Before coming to the region to work in 1983, I knew vaguely that the poet Pablo Neruda had called the narrow band of land between the northern and southern hemispheres the "sweet waist of America." The words resounded when I looked upon valleys veined with silvered streams, or walked about a town plaza centered with an ancient *ceiba* tree filled at dusk with the cries of a thousand starlings. Eventually, to my chagrin, I discovered Neruda had coined the memorable phrase in his great song of the Americas, *Canto General*, in a stanza delivering a divine rant on the spoils of capitalism.

> *When the trumpet sounded everything was ready on earth, and Jehovah handed out the world to Coca-Cola Inc., Anaconda, Ford Motors and other entities: the United Fruit company reserved for itself the juiciest bit, the middle coast of my land, the sweet waist of America, re-christened its lands 'Banana Republics,' and on top of the sleeping dead, the unstill heroes who won greatness, freedom and banners, it set up a comic opera: it alienated choice, bestowed Caesarean crowns, unsheathed envy, brought in the dictatorship of flies.*

Despite its origins, the term remained rooted in my mind as a description positive, *sweet waist of America*, the most apt for what I saw in cornfields terraced onto slopes improbably steep, or trekking in deep jungle. The land glimmered, too, in the most unexpected corners. During drying season, rivulets of red annatto seeds flowed down country roads, peasant growers availing themselves of little-used byways. Invariably, a young girl in a thin cotton dress poked the seeds with a rake so they might dry on all sides, her moves like that of a fire tender tasked with maintaining a glow. The green leaves of coffee bushes shone even in shade, and lakes shimmered lapis or aquamarine, whether from mineral alchemy special to their waters, or a peculiarity of light near the Tropic of Cancer. Even black, it seemed, was the deepest, most resonant black on earth. Lava rock fences, *true black*, and boulders too heavy to move, lying in fields where they had been spat. Once I walked the paths of a mountain town strewn with obsidian like shards of black ice. The eruption that produced them had taken place so long ago, or perhaps the earth had evacuated its store so thoroughly, there was no volcano in sight. Glass remained everywhere for miles, however, black glittering, sharp to the eye.

In Guatemala, the exception to the general vivacity of color was the capital, population 2 million and hazy with pollution. The stinking *basurero,* the metropolitan garbage dump, presented the haziest expanse of all, the size of eight football fields in a natural depression alongside the General Cemetery. The first time I saw the *basurero*, from half a mile away, I thought of the Hieronymus Bosch triptych I had seen once in the Prado, *The Garden of Earthly Delights*, not when the painting is open to the more familiar color and dynamic figures, but the way it looks with its wings closed, when it presents a lifeless circle of earth in tones of gray.

Seen up close, however, the *basurero* was alive. Inhabitants walked around wearing bags on their shoulders, stabbing at objects on the ground with a stick to bring them closer, or bending for inspection, crisscrossing the terrain this way while large vans and trucks came and went marked with the names of hospitals, supermarkets, some with no names at all. Small, scattered flames peppered the ground, triggered, I later found out, by spontaneous combustion or chemical waste, erupting and falling of their own accord, as little noticed, it seemed, as heartbeats.

# RICOCHET

Nancy's *niños fotografos,* eight young photographers, called the dump home. Their garbage collection work was too valuable to their families for them to attend school. Children, small with practiced eyes, might be the first to claim plastic bags, hypodermic needles, half-eaten Big Macs. They grabbed certain items raining down from the trucks even before they hit the ground. Less cautious than adults, however, sometimes a child might be crushed accidentally by a bulldozer, or wait too long to bolt from the path of a garbage truck moving in reverse and fall under its wheels. I went to the *basurero* often after Nancy began with the youngsters and saw how its system worked: families lived in houses cobbled together of discarded metal and strong cardboard, with dirt yards where they sorted finds into piles. They sold the stuff to middlemen working out of sheds on the dump's outer ring, each a specialist in a different trade: plastic bags by color; glass; cans; bedsprings; clothing by gender and size; medicine and other tablets; shoes; shoelaces; heels of shoes; and so on. Youngsters kept found toys and did not give up food of any condition.

Nancy had first come to the *basurero* on assignment with a colleague who was writing about the gritty side of the capital. Children, enchanted by the cameras, swarmed around her, and she let them look through the viewfinders and explained the mechanics of focus and zoom. A Trinidadian nun, one of three who worked with families in the dump, witnessed the scene and asked Nancy if she might return to show the youngsters more, perhaps even give them a class?

Soon Nancy distributed cheap cameras to four girls—one was only age 5 but had to be included because her 8-year-old sister was in the group and the younger could not be left alone—and four boys, the oldest named Rember, a stringy 12-year-old. They met in the house of the Trinidadian nuns.

31.

The first day I visited one of Nancy's classes, I looked out the window across the pall of smoke and saw bundles falling into the dump from the cemetery wall. "Sometimes the graveyard workers toss down remains from old tombs," she explained.

The kids had spread their work on a large table, 8 by 10 photos, black and white, with titles. A woman ("My Mother") scrubbed clothes at an outdoor stone basin; in the background loomed a house wall made from rescued billboard canvas advertising makeup, so that a perfect eye with long lashes watched over the scene, incapable of closing. A scraggle-haired pup ("Negrito") jumped high for a ball coming apart in the air, its rotting rubber skin peeling free. A young woman ("My Aunt on Drugs") stared at the camera amid piles of clothing falling out of open dresser drawers. One photo looked as if it had been shot with a diffusion filter, but it would be years before the children would have such equipment. It showed a panorama in smoke, garbage scavengers standing in a line gazing downward, the point of view original, taken not from in front but behind them ("The Day We Found a Fresh Dead Body in the Dump").

Marta, the five-year-old, a K'iche' Maya indigenous girl who wore the long, native costume of the countryside, had contributed several pictures of adult scavengers, apparently meant to be full portraits, but their heads were lopped off. She was small, even for her age. "You can step back. Or extend your arms to raise the camera," Nancy said to her quietly. Eventually Marta would wear shoes, attend classes, and graduate from university. She would teach in a high school and tutor photographers at a building outside the dump owned by an association created by the young photographers, two floors of offices (as young adults, the kids started their own advertising agency), a digital photography lab, and classrooms. On the day I saw the photos by the original students spread across the wide table, Marta's serious face—it has never changed—responded to the critique with an expression not abashed but attentive.

That day I gave Nancy a ride home. In the 15 minutes it took to cover the distance from the dump to her leafy neighborhood of the capital, she talked about nothing but the promise of one child after another and the low-intensity warfare she was waging against their parents. Marta's mother wanted the sisters to begin looking for work as house servants, a natural fate of Indian girls who come to the city. Others begrudged time the children were taking from the search for trash. I listened with the interest one takes in the life of a friend, not in the conversation. I am sorry to say it, but stories of children in unspeakable circumstances were legion in Guatemala, so that the ear, in general, became dead to them, lest the mind be continually shaken and frayed. Nancy spoke not at all of the wars, so I did not bring up developments. I felt I must say something about the youngsters, however, their pictures I had just seen. They were affecting, documentary and unsentimental, images a professional from the outside would be hard put to replicate.

"They certainly have the access," I said.

In the following months I traveled alone to cover the Guatemalan war that percolated far from the capital and the war in El Salvador, where skirmishes in the countryside and urban death squad attacks were increasing. I shied away from bringing up events to Nancy because they were too sharp to relive with someone who had not been there, someone slipping away from the life.

One day when she was returning to Guatemala from a

visit to the States, I picked Nancy up at the airport and took her straight to the dump, where a class was scheduled. As we slowed before the nuns' house, I saw a boy running toward us wearing frayed-bottom pants a little too short for him, holding his camera with one hand so it wouldn't bounce on the strap he wore around his neck. I recognized Rember, my favorite of the youngsters, perhaps for the mix of eagerness and reflection I always saw in his eyes. And for his evocative name, which called up the word, "Remember."

Nancy stepped out of the car and Rember stood on his toes to throw his arms around her. He seemed to squeeze his eyes against tears. "We thought you would not come back," he said.

The other kids ran up behind him, jumping in place. Nancy grabbed her bag from the backseat and hugged them all and headed for the house, the children following in an exuberance of chatter. I had not yet turned off the engine. She had not said good-bye.

One early morning, too early for a casual call, the phone rang and Nancy's voice said, "It's me."

"Will this be worth five minutes of my time?" I said. It was a response not meant to cut but a way we had; if I called first, she said it. I suppose we thought it was funny, in the way we never signed our own names to notes we wrote to each other, or later, to e-mails, but used signatures like "Evita," "Mata Hari," "Hepburn," or "Gellhorn," never the same name twice.

"Yes," she said. Usually the tip, or the rumor, or the news spilled out then. This time she said nothing.

"So...what's up?" I said.

"It's bad. I think it's bad. I hope it's not bad but I think it might be bad."

"Want me to come?" I asked.

"Would you?"

"I'll be there in an hour," I said. This was not about news, I could tell. "Where are you?"

"Home. We can start from here."

"OK, I'm on my way," I said. "Nance, can you just give me a headline?"

"Rember has disappeared."

I drove the winding road out of the valley of Antigua to the capital, picturing Rember as I had often seen him, the SLR camera around his neck, roaming the dump. He possessed the most documentary eye of all the kids, I thought, grabbing moments that told a wide story, even aspiration, in a single shot. "The Anonymous Couple," seated on a worn granite step, caught in a kiss, the photo cut just below the eyes, so their embrace remained secret. Rember's parents wanted him to go to school, and his older sister wanted to be in the photo class, too, but accepted the norm that only one sibling might participate, lest a family become a target of jealousy, *envidia*.

At her house Nancy was ready to go. "His father called me from the pay phone in the dump, said he hasn't come home for two days," she said. "They're wrecks."

We started the search in a shabby part of town. Nancy and I once had produced a story on murders of street children, so we drove to one of the pockets of the city where we knew they lived. Sometimes runaways, or kids newly tangled up in drugs, attached themselves to kids whose only home was the streets. It did not seem probable Rember would be among them, but it was a place to start, and we parked at the old train station with some hope. Whenever we spotted youngsters who looked bedraggled, we stopped to talk, skipping those who carried plastic bags filled with the yellowish muck of glue. Vapors killed brain cells and altered thinking, allowing a sniffer to forget his troubles but also rendering him incoherent for a time, so you couldn't trust their observations.

Of others we inquired, "Have you seen a 12-year old boy, curly hair, nice smile? He may be dirty, because he disappeared a few days ago. Have you seen someone like that?"

Unsuccessful near the train station, we scoured two parks, one downtown where shoppers and businessmen passed apparently oblivious to the proximate society of urchins, and another, smaller square across from a church behind the National Palace. We watched our backs for the errant mugger, although the kids and homeless men who shared the parks did not seem a threat, at least in the daytime. We had no luck.

At nightfall we cruised a red zone where children, some who looked only seven or eight years old, milled around alleys where prostitutes solicited or served men who never left their cars. We didn't park because even the old Volkswagen would have been stripped for parts in minutes but asked our questions from the windows, rolled down halfway. Nothing. We drove to a block near the National Printing Office, where a couple of pizza joints operated all night, because we knew street kids huddled on the sidewalks against the walls for the warmth from the ovens. Rember was not there.

I slept at Nancy's for what was left of the night. At dawn, Rember's parents called to say a neighbor had reported that the day Rember disappeared he was seen with two boys near a small lake—more like a water-filled ditch—on the extreme southern end of the dump, a corner so far from the area where trucks came in that it was free of trash and looked like open countryside.

At their house in the *basurero*, Rember's mother opened the door quickly. Inside, neighbors sat on the bed and four stools, the only furniture, and more stood. They talked to each other and across each other, an air of solemn watch tempered by chatter. Rember's sister wandered in and out of the only other room, looking around silently with wide, alert eyes that said she might be listening for something outside. Slicing like a rusty saw through it all was an incessant, single voice, an evangelical Christian woman who had perched herself in a corner facing the room, praying aloud nonstop for the boy's return.

Rember's father approached us. "Will you take me to the morgue?" he asked.

He must get out of the house, he said. What he left unsaid, I thought, was that sooner or later he must face the worst possibility. Or eliminate it. When we arrived at the low, concrete block building 15 minutes away, Rember's father wanted to enter alone. It felt uncomfortable to wait for him in the car, watching aggrieved or determinedly composed people walking in and out. Half an hour passed. Rember's father returned looking shaken but reported that his son was not among the unclaimed dead.

The next morning as we sat at the kitchen table drinking coffee, Nancy received another call from the dump. Could we come to Rember's house to pick up his father and uncle? The *bomberos*, volunteer firemen, would tell us where to go from there.

"The *bomberos*?" I said. They were young men trained in search and rescue, most notably to reclaim the remains of death squad victims and other targets of crime. "That means they must have found…"

"Just say it," Nancy said. Why was she impatient and sour with *me*?

"Something," I said. "They must have found something."

We collected Rember's father and his uncle and stopped

at a pay phone to call the *bomberos*. The body of a teenage boy had been discovered on a stream bank about five miles west, deep in a canyon alongside a rivulet that originated in the dump's small lake. The *bombero* team would wait for us on the roadside above the canyon.

In less than 20 minutes the densely populated center of Guatemala City gave way to its scraggly edge. We drove among pines and tiny cornfields, sharing the road with youngsters on horseback and farmers walking with machetes, their pants tucked into rubber boots. A municipal bus climbed ahead of us, riding top-heavy with cardboard boxes and bundles wrapped in brightly woven cloth and huge net bags full of oranges and onions. The bus disappeared around sharp curves tilting so precariously I thought each turn must be its last, but when we followed each time, there it was, upright again, chugging along, expelling black smoke. I saw the *bomberos* and pulled onto the shoulder. The bus drove on.

One young man extracted a circle of ropes from the front seat of their van, looping it over his shoulder, while the other carried what seemed to be a cloth stretcher rolled up between poles. Sometimes volunteers joined the *bomberos* corps because they did not want to carry a gun; the rescue team job kept them out of the army and the paramilitaries. That might have been the motivation of these youths, we couldn't know, but they did act compassionately, assuring Rember's father and uncle that the body reportedly at the bottom of the cliff carried no identification, and the older men might wait more comfortably on the rim. All four descended into the canyon together, however, to recover the remains, no matter whose they were.

As we waited, that singular highland atmospheric called *chippy chippy* rolled in, a misty dampness that blunts the edges of solid objects to the eye, moves hues steps closer to their neutrals on the color scale, muffles sound. Finer than fog, not quite drizzle, the *chippy chippy* softened the look of the world outside the car but threw it out of focus, too. Inside, we waited silently. The bus we had followed on the outward trip passed us on its return. A town, at least a bus stop with a snack stand, must be close ahead. I should take Nancy's mind off things, I thought.

"Shall we try and find some coffee?" I said.

"Yeah, right, and get taken for baby snatchers," she said.

For a moment, I had forgotten. Fear that foreigners were kidnapping children had risen recently, as it did in waves, every few months. Sometimes the trepidation grew into hysteria that caused attacks on tourists, as had happened the week before in a town on the south coast. I chalked up the phenomenon to a visceral response that exploded unpredictably, a reaction to the sight of so many foreigners adopting local infants, or amazement at news that in some places hearts and livers could be transplanted from one human being to another, begging the question, "Might the parts not come from stolen children?" Imagine if a local rabble-rouser up ahead discovered that we, two foreign women, were looking for a young boy and distorted the information. Better to stay in the car.

*Chippy chippy* dropped the temperature. The windshield fogged with our breath. Nancy pulled the collar of her blue sweater higher around her neck, leaned her head back against the seat, and closed her eyes. The sun was still visible in gray air, a coin in the sky, its color off, like a zinc penny you still sometimes found in the States, the kind used during World War II when copper was scarce. I stared, attempting to detect actual movement of the orb on its arc. I remembered reading that staring directly at the sun, for even a short time, can damage the eyes. Some years hence, I thought, I might look back, remembering these hours spent inside a silent car, and consider, *that's when I started to go blind.*

Perhaps the body the men would recover would not be Rember. Maybe he was home now, I thought, the lark over, expecting a hiding from his father but proud of himself for a first solo foray into the world, anxious to show off the pictures he took beyond the circle of the dump. *Do not run this scenario by Nancy or she will throw that look that says you have fallen out of the saddle.* I was deeply sorry for my friend; if I dreaded bad tidings about Rember, a boy I found especially endearing and full of life, how much more Nancy must be feeling. But perhaps the experience of these days would convince her that she was out of her element, that it was time to return to the job. And we could work together again. I was ashamed to be thinking selfishly at such a time, but I forgave myself, too. How would I go on without her?

I tapped a finger softly but incessantly on the steering wheel. She stirred.

"Sleeping?" I said.

She shook her head.

*Of course not.*

The edges of the windows shone iridescent with age and acidic pollution and rubber leaching from their trim. I cleared a circle on the driver's side with my hand.

"See anything?" she asked, startling me with her voice.

"No," I said. I had been waiting for her to break the silence so we might truly talk, but when she did, I could say only, "Nothing."

Nancy splayed her hands on the dashboard and looked at them. I noticed her nails were bitten to the quick. She must bite them when she is asleep, I thought, because I have never seen her bite her nails. Or maybe she does bite them in the daytime, and I never noticed. There are things I do not know about her, I thought.

"I left because I did not want any more of death," she said.

"We don't know," I said. She was assuming Rember was dead. I wasn't sure she was talking to me.

"I left because I wanted to do something that would make a difference, even in one or two lives, when it didn't seem I was making any difference by taking the pictures."

I heard what I had not wanted to hear before. Nancy was on the lifetime plan here. Something in her voice said she would make no more changes, that she would not come back to our work, that she would stick it out.

"Remember the Torola River?" I said. Usually just the phrase raised a smile, recalling the time we had come under fire midstream and crawled in the water back to shore to rise out of the river in our underwear, surprising troops just long enough so they stopped shooting and someone gave an order to request instructions from headquarters, saving our sorry hides.

"Remember the Torola?" I tried.

Through the scrim of moist air, the men appeared over the rim of the canyon, carrying the stretcher, the shape of a body shrouded on the pallet. Rember's father and uncle held the poles front and back on the right side, the firemen on the left. They walked toward the *bomberos*' van about 30 feet away from us. Nancy rubbed a clear round on the windshield and leaned forward to peer through it.

"Shall we go?" I asked, my hand on the door.

"I don't need to go," she said.

"But..."

"I don't need to go," she said sharply, still looking through the cleared spot. Then more softly, "It's him."

"How do you know?"

In a cruel instant I knew the answer, that she knew the same way I would know if the form on the stretcher were—God forbid, I thought, and closed my eyes—my own daughter.

The men slipped the stretcher into the van. Rember's father looked toward us and lifted a hand slowly, less a wave than a salute, then put his knee on the floor of the van and crawled inside. Nancy raised her hand and kept it in the air a moment after he disappeared.

"We can go now," she said.

I took hold of the wheel and she put her hand on mine. "Thanks for coming with me," she said.

"Hey," I said, making a U-turn. "Home?"

"No," she said. "The kids will be waiting at the classroom. I want them to hear this from me."

It is a truism that we remember where we were, exactly what we were doing, at the moment we received news of a transcendent historical event. I was sitting in a parked car on a dark street with my high-school boyfriend, discussing his upcoming deployment to Vietnam, where two of our fellow classmates had already lost their lives, when the radio announced that President Kennedy had been assassinated. On a January morning in 1986, I was racing up the back stairs to the second floor of the El Camino Real when a colleague from the *Washington Post*, coming the other way, told me to slow down, because news from Central America would not find space that day. "*Challenger* exploded," he said. Only a month before, when I had discovered I was pregnant, I had rescinded my NASA application—one of tens of thousands, I expect—to be a "Journalist in Space" but continued to follow the story of the *Challenger*'s "Teacher in Space," Christa McAuliffe. I recall how my hand went to my belly at news of the disaster. I heard first of 9/11 from an indigenous Maya scholar in a mountain village in Guatemala, who asked me to accept his condolences for the souls lost in the buildings crumbling in my country and planes falling out of its skies.

For all the precision with which I remember my whereabouts at such pivotal moments, despite efforts I cannot remember exactly when I heard of the fall of the Berlin Wall, even though it marks the most significant historical event in my lifetime. The wall was more than bricks; for as long as I had been a journalist it had been the symbol of the Manichaean struggle between global forces, putatively black and white, good and frightful, lands and movements presumptively in the orbit of the United States or the Soviet Union. When the wall came down and the Cold War ground to an end, the struggle against Communism—where it had been real, or falsely ascribed to inconvenient insurrections—disappeared from Washington's political agenda, soon to be couched in terms of terrorism. My heart was in Latin America, and my growing girl, it seemed, was a natural part of the place and should not be uprooted. I watched my colleagues depart for Bosnia, Iraq, Afghanistan as if watching the change of a rich season, not with regret that I did not follow, but knowledge that such a time would not come again.

Unless I look up the date, however, I recall only vaguely that the Berlin Wall fell after the men found Rember dead; sometime around the most violent days of the war in El Salvador; just before or just after the night of my daughter's first dance recital, in which she performed wearing a pink kimono; and definitely before the last U.S. military action of the Cold War, the invasion of Panama. I attribute my imprecise recollection to the avalanche of duties and emotions in those weeks, the confounding accumulation of life in the nine months since Nancy had first said to me, "I just can't take another picture of a dead body."

Rember's sister, who joined Nancy's photography class after her brother's death, insisted on leading the others in an excursion to take pictures of his tomb, but Nancy did not want to come. On a bright morning I drove five kids to the corner of the General Cemetery where Rember lay interred in a white wall among other cubicles sealed with cement, or gaping still vacant and dark. Nearby, beyond rows of graves in the ground, the dump lay in its vale, producing the acrid smell that wafted over the young photographers as they worked, an odor not overwhelming but inescapable. Rember's cause and manner of death remained unknown, at least Nancy did not want to talk about it if she did know, but I figured it was a murder spurred by *envidia*, that devastating form of jealousy, the crime of the weak turned mean. Or perhaps it was a simple theft gone violent when the boy would not give up his camera. Rember's sister came out of the grief that had gripped her since her brother's death by throwing herself almost fanatically into the photo class. "She wants to be a journalist," Nancy told me. "She actually chases fire engines." The girl was 13. I had seen her do it. On foot.

About nine months after the Salvadoran elections, on November 11, 1989, the Farabundo Martí National Liberation Front guerrillas surprised the capital in El Salvador, attacking military targets and occupying entire neighborhoods, traversing even wealthy enclaves like Escalon, with its potted window plants and carports. A U.S.-trained army unit, on orders from the generals, assassinated six priests who believed in a negotiated—not military—solution to the violence, also killing their housekeeper and her daughter. Where ordinary Salvadorans were not huddling under their beds for shelter from bullets and mortars, they were moving along streets in tight, frightened groups bearing white flags, carrying small children and what household goods they might, looking for safety. I called Nancy from San Salvador.

"I know you don't want to cover news any more," I said. "But you should come. This is the big one."

A few days later she was one of the few reporters to penetrate the luxurious Sheraton Hotel when it came under siege by guerrillas, trapping several members of the U.S. Delta Force, who had been called in to assist the Salvadoran army. Her pictures: the U.S. soldiers barricaded in a guest room with M16s and sidearms; guerrilla sharpshooters at windows in a staircase, firing out. Besides the American military, the siege rendered dozens of other foreigners hostage, including the secretary-general of the Organization of American States, João Baena Soares, who had come to mediate a solution to the war (all were safely released). One picture depicted the global functionary looking alarmed but dignified at a point when the outcome of the siege was still in doubt. The Sheraton was a headline incident and Nancy's coverage far better than mine. (I never reached the hotel's front door, hunkered instead across the street behind a low garden wall for the duration of the drama, pinned down by sharpshooter fire.) It was her last frontline story.

Less than three weeks later, I rose to a predawn call from San Francisco. "Turn on your television," said my editor's voice. "Time to go." He is British. In the dark, in my groggy state, his phrases sounded taken from a James Bond movie.

"What's up?" I said.

"The eagle has landed."

"What? What time is it?"

"Midnight in Panama."

On the screen U.S. aircraft flew, building walls exploded. Tracers crisscrossed the night sky, creating incandescent lace; even on TV their whistling pierced the skull. On the streets, leaping young men, and women running with children in their arms, were silhouettes against backdrops of fire. The news crawl read, "Operation Just Cause."

Later Nancy told me her first impulse had been to enter Panama with the rest of us who made flights that morning. By this time, however, sales from the children's photos and donations from friends had allowed her to buy shoes and school uniforms. The U.S. invasion coincided with the period of signing up kids from the dump for schools and convincing hesitant—even recalcitrant—parents that school in fact was a good thing. In the end she had to lay down a rule, that only children who attended—they were crazy for the idea—might continue with the photography classes. The first day of the U.S. invasion of Panama (2,106 civilians died or disappeared in its four-day duration) was the very day Nancy must accompany a girl who had never been to school before, and her single mother, to registration. How could she miss that event?

I got a page one story out of Panama, and several inside page stories, and would have stayed to look for follow-up features had I not promised my daughter and her father that I would be home for Christmas. I arrived on the morning of December 24. That evening we picked up Nancy and drove to a hilltop house above the lights of Guatemala City. Inside, tables sparkled with plates of pate and ceviche and bottles of imported wine. The host held a U.S. Embassy position; his wife played the piano for carols. I felt as if I were singing in a dream, where I could not hear my own voice. My daughter in a red velvet dress, looking as if she had stepped from a Victorian greeting card, stood close to the piano so she could see the keys; I placed my hand on her shoulder for ballast, because I felt unsteady in the cinnamon air. The glass of the room's picture windows reflected bright baubles and flaring candle tongues, so the view beyond became a city burning, like Panama.

When the music stopped, I decided I could not talk about the invasion with Nancy, who was telling guests about

# RICOCHET

registering the youngsters for school. Around us, revelers wore the oversize rhinestone jewelry and silk neckties covered with elves that Christmas brings out. When someone mentioned that I had just returned from Panama, a guest I did not know said, "That one was fast, wasn't it?"

I walked to the den to be alone, but the host's elderly father was there, watching television. "Sit, sit," he said.

I stood, watching Panama City on the news, the wrecked parts. The old man turned in his leather lounge chair. "The war," he said, as if all war were one.

I could not have known then, but I might have guessed, that Nancy and I would continue to be friends 25 years later, although I have not felt that peculiar connection with her that friendship under fire can bring since the night she told me, "I just can't take another picture of a dead body," and our paths split. I could not have known then, but believe I would not have been surprised, that her first class of child photographers would grow into classes that would count hundreds. That they would visit Tokyo, London, and many other places with exhibits, take jobs in art or journalism or teaching new generations of small photographers from the dump, and from shacks along the railroad tracks, and faraway villages, and that many would graduate from university. And others, like Rember, unable to survive circumstances, would die before their time. I watch Nancy today busy with the project, still concerned about funding, and about the young people's worries—an alcoholic uncle, an unplanned pregnancy—but I believe she does see the effects on lives of the time she has put in, the decisions she made, although she would not say it that way.

Once, I believed the work of placing true observations before the eyes of readers was enough for good to triumph, and for evil, or misbegotten policy, to be acknowledged, so it might disappear. I still believe the bones and sinews of war must be observed and recorded, as intimately as possible. About the rest, I am no longer sure.

# RICOCHET

## About the Author

Mary Jo McConahay is the author of *Maya Roads, One Woman's Journey Among the People of the Rainforest* (Chicago Review Press). She is an award-winning journalist and documentary filmmaker whose coverage of war, politics, and international justice issues over three decades has appeared in Time, Newsweek, the Los Angeles Times, Vogue, Rolling Stone, and dozens of other newspapers and magazines. Also a believer in writing "deep travel," weaving local history and voices into narrative, she has been honored as the Lowell Thomas Travel Journalist of the Year, a distinction considered equivalent to the Pulitzer Prize in the genre. She is currently writing a book about World War II in Latin America, scheduled for publication in 2018 by St. Martin's Press (Macmillan).

Recognition for *Maya Roads* includes the Northern California Book Award for Best Nonfiction Book, National Geographic Traveler Book of the Month, Society of American Travel Writers Grand Award, Independent Publisher's Award for Best Travel Essay Book, Los Angeles BookNews International Book Awards for Best New Nonfiction Book, Best Travel Essay Book, and Best Memoir/Autobiography.

*Ricochet, Two Women War Reporters and a Friendship under Fire* is also available as an ebook from Shebooks.net and as an audiobook from Audible.com, or from Amazon.com.

*Mayaroads.com*
*Maryjomcconahay.net*

www.ingramcontent.com/pod-product-compliance
Lightning Source LLC
Chambersburg PA
CBHW052030290426
44112CB00014B/2457